To .

The

Hop

lite-, you -

Jonny

Frisking the Betweens

John Hulme

May 2024

Frisking the Betweens

by John Hulme

First paperback edition

ISBNs:
Paperback: 978-1-80541-526-8
ebook: 978-1-80541-527-5

Contents

little still piece

Sometimes I'm scared I have drifted too far

from every gorgeous thing you do.

There are days

when I want to bottle

every act of kindness . . .

every laugh . . .

every moment of understanding . . .

every connection . . .

There are days

when I want to bottle them all

before the nasty stuff

tries to take them down.

There are days,

lost lives buttered into moments,

where

all I want to do is

pick them up

and throw them into the tide,

the river . . .

the rain,

rolling down a street that will not stop –

unlike me,

frozen as I am.

I'll stop right here.

I'll stop right now,

just for the wave I didn't see coming,

weeping ashore as your face starts to dance.

Over me?

I'll wait forever out in space –

even when the ships all burn,

the shores all shatter

and the world won't turn.

I'll wait in the glow of that one sacred space.

I'll wait here for all of those pieces of you

and every precious thing you do.

Small venue

The sky is discovering new hues of blue,

as yellow things wither

and weep on the horizon,

the way yellow things have always done.

Wading birds frisk the treasure-peppered beach for new flight.

Clouds power up on moonbeams,

glowing their way into small orbits . . .

hovering like alien ships.

All these things

and

me,

so small and insignificant in your scheme of things,

where

everything is measured against something bigger.

Yet here I am,

steering an invasion

from the secret galaxy over the bay.

Rivulet battalions are retreating with the tide,

leaving my silence to negotiate a truce.

All this for a moment in your arms,

I whisper.

Vast,

billowy tentacles,

spring-loaded from the rains,

loaded with planet-killer orange from distant sunsets . . .

They stir the whirlpool where my spirit leaks free,

considering my offer.

Tomorrow, we'll play again,

purring between all the grander venues where space remains
empty.

Impossible

My name's John.

I have my own little language.

It's not one I can speak, which is quite odd considering it's been my language for so much of my life.

But truly, it's an impossible language to speak sometimes –

which is ironic, because it's the language that explains (if that isn't too analytical, too rational, too damn prescriptive a word) why some days are simply impossible for me.

Some days. Some weeks. Some months. Some years, truth be told.

I guess I'm making it sound like a silent language, because clearly other people don't get to hear me not being able to speak it.

But it's not. It's like a scream, dug out from caves deep beneath the ocean – my ocean,

the one I carry with me,

the one that anyone can come and explore and swim in for the price of a smile and some crazy linguistic curiosity.

It's like me on all my worst days, writing something that only spills out in my best moments –

and in those magic words, you can see all the incredible misadventures that link the two together.

You can see what it actually means to be human . . .

to be authentic.

They're not smug words.

They're not judgemental or authoritarian.

They're not in the least self-righteous –

partly because they claim nothing to be righteous about,

partly because they have no wish to bully anyone.

They have no wish to be competitive either.

They just float and hover there, like clouds in a freezing late-evening sky, looking for someone who gets it . . .

whose heart has been forged in the same lens . . .

who sees the stories.

It's a language nobody speaks yet.

It's a language nobody wants, standing in front of a world that has often felt impossible.

It's feeling impossible for me right now.

Saying this, what I actually want, need to say . . .

that's impossible too.

It's already terrified – if a floating voiceless language can claim to be terrified – of the comments and replies that saying this might elicit.

That goes with the territory, I'm afraid.

But that doesn't matter. If you tear me down at this point, you'll be adding nothing to the story.

You'll be adding nothing to the unspoken language.

The only way to do that is to learn a language we've never spoken before,

right now,

in that place where perhaps some of you are standing as you read this,

lost in a world that's turned impossible . . .

trying to remember all the tiniest things about being human . . .

all the things tingling in the cracks of your heart right now,

trying to bridge the impossible.

Light of the rain bear

The roof of the cabin was dancing drumbeats into the heavy wet air.

Any other time, I might have enjoyed the sheet immersive intensity of it, boxed into the dark core of a storm. But not this time; not with my head throbbing and screaming, the dull aches tumbling down my arms and my chest stinging with tiny pieces of sharp, twisted glass.

Thick rivers rolled out of my eyes. Thick wet juggernauts.

I couldn't speak, even if there was anyone left for me to talk to. My phone buzzed on the table as an email arrived from somebody I didn't have either the heart or the stomach to reply to. I needed a miracle of some kind. I needed the kind of miracle that had long-since stopped believing in itself.

I was starting to melt into the rug when the door burst open.

The big brown bear hung in the doorway, its head swaying like a furry pendulum.

"It's too scary out there," it sighed, in a sad, snuffly and, so it seemed to me at least, a very unbearlike voice.

The smell of wet bear swooshed into the room with the hail of raindrops from its massive shaking head, and my own head was screaming louder than ever as one of those massive paws swung the door shut again.

"I wish I knew what to say," snuffled the bear, lowering its massive snout so that it could nuzzle my face with that shockingly gentle touch you can only hope for in an unexpected talking animal.

"I am boiling over with gazillions of things I want to say," it continued, "but I just can't find it in me to speak."

I wanted to say it seemed to be doing pretty well to me, but on this occasion, I had to admit to being way more dumbstruck than the bear.

"I want to rip out a piece of sky, and smear it with my heart. I want to beam something beautiful clear across the star plains, and split the oceans open until huge herds of sea monsters spill out over these mountains.

"Instead, I feel . . . scared . . . and lost . . . a big, lumbering ghost of a thing, wondering who . . . or what . . . I really am."

We stared into each other's eyes like explorers on an unfamiliar shore, neither of us feeling insightful enough to see quite where we needed to go – perhaps neither of us feeling strong enough to look.

I could see scars glistening between the bear's fur, where old blood flows had crystallised into stained-glass. Eerie light shone out from the churning beast at its core, and I realised we were not do different under the skin.

Its shaggy, storm-sodden claws rested on my shoulder like a couple of counter-intuitive asteroids landing on a lonely spaceship. Each set of claws was bigger than my head, and I could tell this bear was looking for more doors to smash open . . . more raging oceans to fall into.

But all I saw in its eyes was the benevolence of something that knew what it meant to stand alone in the rain with a light the world seemed unable to see.

For all our combined shipwrecks, this shared moment of understanding was probably the most beautiful voyage either of us had taken in a very long time.

Comfort zones

Storm clouds are stalking the ridges – a lion in billow,

gloating over lush green flanks. *Watch out for those comfort zones,* they say,

as the high rocks dissppear behind the rain. The street turns into ballet –

pirouetting puddles everywhere –

as all my landscapes ride out on the river, galloping down to the sea.

Don't stick to your comfort zones, they say.

Don't hide . . .

and all my landscspes roll out like barrels on the tide, fighting the waves

with sea spray swords and

slaying the dragons

as they burrow headless into healing tunnels made of sand. The world is exploding,

just as it did in all those comfort zones I ever thought I owned, before the street

crawled in all my windows

and dragged a closet full of safe places out into traffic.

This is a world of dirty greys and waterfalls,

crashing out between a hundred overlapping skies – stealing the reds

and browns

and all those restless dancing greens . . . hoisting my treasures far out to sea.

I'm barely a heartbeat from running away, following all my stowaway landscapes deep into planets

that orbit in plankton fire and flood.

I'm barely a heartbeat from being a pirate one more time . . . and you talk to me of comfort zones.

Hoodie song

Just as it had done in every other village down the coast, the incoming tide was uncoiling itself, lifting itself into towering, quivering tentacles that loomed over the beach. They swayed this way and that, scanning the seafront with eerie beams of phosphorescence.

I knew this was my fault. It had to be.

I had a notebook packed with doodles and scribbled descriptions of these searchlight serpents, as I called them. I had been writing about them and sketching them for months now, long before I ever saw the things.

Who else could have summoned these creatures?

If that's what they were, of course. Creatures . . . phantoms . . . tidal ghosts . . . echoes of distant horizons und undiscovered worlds, perhaps.

They burrowed their way shoreward with the roll of incoming tide, bursting out of the exploding surf to join the unearthly chorus. That noise they made – the high-pitched screeching that seemed to hover in the air . . . it never began with the serpents. It started with the hoodies.

All along the promenade, leaning into the railings and stretching their cowl-like heads into the darkening air, the hoodie people were howling their disconcerting chorus into sea spray and sparkly, smoky searchlights.

I was watching them from the relative safety of the car, listening to the dialogue of screeches and howls. No words, of course. However eloquent they might have been in their human form, none of the things down on the promenade ever spoke – at least, not in any manner which their old selves would have recognised as speaking. Not once the hoodies had a grip on them.

The surf song never failed to make my skin crawl, and I had wound the windows shut so I wouldn't have to feel the way the salty air danced in its presence.

The car radio came on of its own accord, even though the key was not in the ignition, and I could hear the symphony of screeches crackling over the speakers. Like it or not, I would be hearing the latest triumph of the searchlight serpents.

They needed me to know. They needed me to experience.

This should have been one village too many. It should have broken me. But luckily for me, if not for the rest of the village, I had my own phantom to comfort me. I had you. I could feel your spirit nuzzling me protectively from the passenger seat.

Thank you, I found myself thinking. *Thank you for staying with me, for helping me ride out the nightmare.*

Thank you for being my lifeline.

Was it your lingering presence that had put such fire into my notebook? Was it your presence that had conjured such wild imaginings from those pages? I knew for certain it was my writing that had summoned these monsters. I knew for certain it was my notebook they were following, town by town, village by village, as I fled along the coast, dragging the curse of the searchlights with me.

But I still had no real idea why.

I never thought I would miss the rhythms of idle chatter quite so much. How could I have thought this town would be any different?

These people should have been my friends. For the first time in my long drift along the coast, I had very nearly touched souls other than the one that was haunting me. Living, breathing souls, with simple, human stories to tell.

I had started to forge something resembling genuine friendship again – and in my arrogance, I had assumed the thawing of my isolation, the loosening of alien ties on my heart, might have halted the march of searchlights across the coastline.

But no.

The sinister vigil of the hoody folk would be widening a little tonight, and a little more of the coast would be lost.

I watched the line of villagers as they swayed together along the promenade railings. The misty fabric of their hoodies pulsed and glowed beneath the searchlights. It breathed. It sang. It screamed into the thick, churning water.

I wondered if anything human remained beneath those hoods . . . and I thought back to all the other places I had stayed . . . all the other places that had ended up the same way. "Why?"

I expected no answer, but the question spilled out anyway. "Why are you following me?"

What was it about these hungry words of mine, these strange, uncomfortable words of loss and yearning, that had drawn them. Why had I been chosen as their beacon?

I picked up the notebook, leafing through the poems and sketches and scribbled meditations. In the shadow of that unearthly song on the radio, their restless moments of inspiration began to tingle on the paper, burning like lightning through my fingers . . .

dripping tiny stars over the upholstery . . .

and I thought of lonely sea serpents, sniffing the coastal air for some kind of somewhere to rest their own aching, swim-weary spirits.

I had always imagined the seas to be something unfathomably magical, blessed by all manner of swirling, living galaxies, flying with squadrons of gill-fuelled miracles. But perhaps now, poisoned and overfished as they had been for so many years, there was too much pain and loneliness there, desperate for the kind of intimacies which, however unfairly, seemed always to land on human shoulders.

I began to sense something of the envy such creatures might feel . . . something of the *rage*.

I thought how unbearably cold those depths might seem, once you'd fought your writhing, coiling body high through the currents to find yourself towering among the clouds, gleaming in the moonlight.

I thought about how pretty each of these coastal communities must have looked from the sea, what pretty fires their streetlights made, luring the dispossessed in from the sea.

I had never fully understood this need of mine – this desperation to find words for things that so often felt better left unsaid . . . almost as though the pages were stealing something that might perhaps have belonged somewhere far, far better.

"*It does belong somewhere better,*" hissed a harsh voice from the speaker of the car stereo. "*It belongs with us.*"

I shuddered violently at the unexpected voice.

That was when I realised they really were listening to me . . . to my thoughts.

I dropped the notebook on the passenger seat, and stared at your photograph, stuck to the cover to remind me what love felt like.

I remembered us talking by the railings in a place very similar to this, wrapped in each other's currents as the spray-peppered breeze caressed our bare arms and pressed damp denim against our legs.

I remembered the warmth of your breath on my cheek, and the fire of your words in my soul, the gentle twitching of your skin, invigorated by sea spray after a day of stifling summer sweat.

I remembered your smile, bubbling all the way up to your eyes. I remembered your tears.

Most of all, I remembered my own, following me everywhere with the memory of those hugs, even as your lingering spirit tried so hard to placate me.

That was when I saw the deep dark shadow fall across the windscreen; one of the searchlight serpents, reaching over the promenade railings and peering into the car like some curious reanimated plesiosaur.

It sniffed the glass, clearly hungry for all the precious secrets on the other side.

I fished the lighter from my pocket, flicked on the flame and held it to the notebook. The creature let out a deafening howl – an excruciating, unearthly wail, steeped in pain.

As it reared up, I revved the engine, screeched around the boatyard and sped off towards the coastal road.

That was the last time I felt your presence at my shoulder, the last time your ghost felt real to me.

I think perhaps you're waiting for me to do the right thing – to destroy this cursed notebook before the serpents start to sniff out more hidden treasure from the margins.

Burn it.

Throw it into the sea so the monsters can have it.

Anything to stop this nameless horror from stealing more of the coastline. Deep down, I know it's probably the only way.

But there's so much of you in this book, and so little of me anywhere else. Besides, I know you'll come back to me.

Any day now, I'll look down at your picture and feel your fingers drift once more across my cheek. I'll look up at the clouds and feel the world start to re-paint itself in your presence.

I am spellbound – and we both know it.

I have found another little village where I feel at home, and have found myself inspired to write again, to make new friends with the stories of those around me, and I know it's only a matter of time before the surf cobras come again.

So you tell me . . . how many villages can I sacrifice before you stop forgiving me?

Moss rockets

I want to wander where the gentle things play.

I want to walk

where paths are soft and rich and bright,

vibrant in texture and in palette.

I want to feel kindness,

tender like the whisper of a stream.

I want to be hugged and cuddled again, fuelled

by the passion of vulnerable things,

launching their rockets where the trees once stood . . .

diving into unfamiliar skies

and pulling the miracles back to my heart.

Thick mossy mittens,

rippling

over gnarly tree-stump claws

and flying saucers,

hovering deep in bark-drawn skies.

I want to wander where the gentle things play,

on all those

chilly platforms,

waiting for overcrowded trains

to one last place I've not yet been.

I want to walk

where paths are kind and bricks are bright,

lighting those

sad,

forgotten streets

and windows where moss fingers trace out the rain

and rooms where the saucer ships crumble and die.

I want the whisper that warms me right through,

and

I want the cheap streets to feel these worlds too.

Backpacker

I was so very lost back then . . .

and it seemed as though I was always running –

running through a place that seems in some ways now to exist only in the fevered storm clouds of my imagination. But I know it was real. I lived its realness. I nearly crumbled to dust through the hard, rough fingers of its realness.

I was recklessly, bottomlessly hurt back then.

Everywhere I looked, the world appeared to be sprouting atrocities. Huge ones that blotted out the sky. Small shadowy ones that stole the sound out of heartbeats

All around me, it seemed people were hurting for all the wrong reasons,

and wherever I stood, even the broadest smiles were just a hair-trigger away from dying.

I was lost in a world that I knew could turn on any one of us without warning.

A world that can make you nothing.

A world that can strip all value from your name and march your family into an internment camp,

sanction your benefits,

bomb your cities,

freeze your heart,

machete your children,

throw you in a gas chamber,

cut off your power, your water . . .

put up a fence of guns around your dreams

or simply drive your entire neighbourhood into those dark little woods where the trees speak bullets . . .

for no other reason than your face doesn't fit.

A world that can choose to exterminate your identity simply because the tide is turning that way.

I needed to wash clean of it, before the last of my soul dissolved.

But I had some atrocities of my own to come to terms with. I had blades and thorns inside me, sticking to the wheels and the cogs and the gears as they spun me from footstep to footstep, looking for that authentic place to stand in.

I was a rusted, creaking mechanism, woven from the softest, most vulnerable of hopes.

I was a thing that ought not to have worked, rolling down a road fresh with runaway tears and galloping rivers.

I was the dream of raindrops, soaked into walking shoes.

I was what it means to be human, just long enough to share the revelation of it with the rain.

I was more right than I had ever been, and I had never felt so sadly, spectacularly wrong.

With so many voices screaming their rightness into the abyss, how could I find the love that makes it okay to be so wrong?

To do that, I would have to distil the essence of a love that is deeper, more profound and more accommodating than anything this world could possibly allow.

I would have to shine a love that withers in its own light . . .

a love that cries

freely

in places where it almost feels inhuman to cry –

places so torn and twisted that even tears are beyond us.

And what then would such love say to us, in the midst of all this filth?

How would such love respond to such horror?

Perhaps simply by holding all the terrors of a filthy, scary, nasty world in shattered, vulnerable hands –

hands that, miraculously, could still nurse my broken mechanism through all those rivers and footsteps.

I can't see my way through all the pain and injustice and cruelty and misery. I can barely see my way through my own, however big they tell me my heart is.

I can't conjure that kind of love. "But maybe I can,"

says the backpacker, riding all those teardrops . . . rekindling rivers that nobody ever suspected were there,

tumbling down cosmic river valleys from the massive scary
mountains of the human heart, carrying a backpack full of
broken worlds.

What are you? I wonder,

looking into the backpacker's eyes.

I see the paintwork of galaxies turning there, wheels of cloud lit
by candles too numerous to name,

and I see the poetry that knows them all.

So I find myself hugging something that would likely disappear,
the moment I try to package it, or explain it, or give it a name.

I find myself hugging something that crumbles between my
fingers,

just like those waterfalls crashing down from the clifftops.

Suddenly,

the straps break,

and all those broken worlds begin to fall like morning rain
around the backpacker's feet.

Like waves

Could you share the silence

when I cry?

Could you be with me?

Could you be here,

holding vigil in my eyes,

my heart?

Skate the window glass with me,

smearing

all those mirrors in the rain.

Could you share who I am?

Even when none of me works anymore –

an engine,

stilled in post-war rust,

bombed by the demons that haunt out my heart.

Just enough lines left to hear myself shake

over a network

of shackles

and chain-link

and tie-me-down straps;

just enough to stir my stories right out of the sky.

Could you hold me as I fall?

Dropping

like a stone invader,

whittled

out of solar dust

and fire . . .

dancing

the last of my hope

over all those broken,

quake-torn clouds . . .

diving

right

out of the street lamps –

and landing where the heartache grows.

I'm a hole in the fabric,

a tear in the sky;

a place only stories can whisper.

Talk me into all those things –

all those places I can't go . . .

all those people I can't be . . .

all those things there wasn't a door into.

Talk me

into windows

far

too small

for me to smash

and

hill roads

far too steep for me to climb

and rain

that

just

keeps

pouring

down . . .

even when there's nothing left to drown.

Talk me into

cute little words

I can

play with.

Talk me into drifting free,

rolling

and breathless

and frightened and pure,

like the scars on a painting,

catching themselves on a colour we missed.

Talk me

into writing this

and

help me lift the pen,

carved as it is out of dark cosmic stone,

fallen through the streetlights

and dredged up from the stars,

along with

every other place I've been

between

doorways

that never blew open

and

shop fronts

and

cafes

and

stations

and

warm steaming mugs

on a chilly grey day

and hot spicy nibbles

and freshly-baked cakes,

served on a tray

on the edge of the sky,

and

empty

moonlit

platforms

where the trains all run

on crazy, space-lit poetry.

hanging

on

the

tip

of something my tongue is yearning to be

if I could walk through the things

my breath wants to say

before all the best of them wither away.

Talk me into braiding you –

downstream

like a lover's hair,

weaving the magic we wanted to live

somewhere and elsewhere

but not anywhere.

Talk me back to who you saw;

talk me back to who I was . . .

stitch by stitch

and cog by cog,

the gears

of an old-fashioned clockwork,

tight

on my ribs

where I can't get to sleep

and driven in far too,

far too deep . . .

and

I'll whisper the fuel out of streetlights,

catching the smoke

if the world still turns

and whittling the starships

right where it burns

and

I'll power the heart of my missions

out

through a braided chain of suns

and I'll wander the dark side of freedom,

like waves on a coastal path would do.

The noise of a dark thing

I could hear it rolling in from the horizon – the noise of a dark thing.

A pounding, banging thing, like the steady advance of enemy artillery; like charges being strategically detonated across the midnight sky, the eerie portent of a vast explosion. Something timeless it was, as much a part of our primeval backstory as our future, like a weary, growling dinosaur, pounding its claws over the shimmering horizon.

For some reason, I still had reception on my hand phone. For some reason, even when all the usual channels had fallen silent and all the established transmitters had tumbled into dust, there was still some vestige of a signal on my phone. A phantom network. A dinosaur's roar, perhaps, woven through the crazy magnetics of a torn sky.

It didn't even sound like a phone call. It sounded . . . *felt* like her. Like she was here with me on the edge of the abyss.

"Where are you?" she asked.

"Out on the shore," I replied, listening to the echoes roll and ripple overhead.

"Don't do this to yourself," she pleaded. "What good will it do, taking yourself off like this? Does it make you feel any stronger, staring into the inevitable, all on your own? Hell, you've felt it coming longer than any of us! What's the use of torturing yourself now?"

"And the others?" I asked, trying to imagine the mood back at the camp. "Have *they* stopped torturing each other?"

She sighed into the silence between oncoming drumbeats.

"They've been drinking and talking round the fire all night, saying the same things they said last night . . . how hopeless it all is, how useless. How nobody is coming to our rescue. How we brought this all on ourselves."

I sighed heavily at the familiarity of her words. "Almost like . . ."

I sighed again, trying and failing to choke back the sobs.

"No, go on!" she insisted.

"Almost like they're enjoying the bleakness of it," I ventured.

"Yes . . . In a way, yes . . . just that. They're almost . . . they're almost *competing* with each other in their knowingness, sharing their certainties, their grim philosophies about how nobody is coming to save anybody. You know the spiel: how we are all woven meaninglessly from a swirl of random, heartless things, and then drained by the very mechanism that created us."

I knew the creed. Most of those at the camp wore it like a badge of honour as the skies got darker and darker.

"What a tragic little language of self-sabotage we've invented for ourselves," she said.

Perhaps we were the real dark thing after all, summoning monsters from a sky that, given half a chance, might have preferred to be our friend.

I tried to take a breath, only to stumble in the attempt. More sobs began to catch in my throat, drawing on a childlike sadness that refused to go away, even in a world where there appeared to be nothing left to cry for.

Overhead, moonlight glinted through a billowy crack in the clouds. A frozen spark across the sky, glowing with weird magnetospheric angst. Phosphorescent space plankton, sparking their flinted crystal bodies against cosmic rays. Whatever they were, they knew how to catch my mood. I felt the memory of so many magnificent stories in their floating flame . . .

so many spectacular campfires, swimming in the blue-black silence, defying the noise of a dark thing we always knew would come for us one day.

"Look, it makes no odds what you feel," she snarled, suddenly losing patience with a coldness that wasn't really her – a coldness she felt she'd been forced to adopt by a world where the lights had gone out.

"Whatever we did, whatever difference we tried to make, it's all being swept away now, isn't it? Everything we held on to will be torn to shreds when that sky comes down on us. You're nothing but a tiny thing in the path of a massive wave, and you know that. Like I said before, you've known it far longer than any of us. It's been seeping out of your bones for years, the knowledge of it. I think knowing it broke your heart before you even knew what it meant to have a heart."

There was a bitter edge to her words now, an edge of accusation. I knew the place it came from, and I couldn't blame her. In truth, I felt it too.

But I still couldn't go back to camp. Not tonight. Not even in the knowledge that there wouldn't be any other nights.

"So ok, you go sit on your beach, then!" she yelled. "If that's what you want, you go and play with your poems one last time. Bathe in the sunrise that's never gonna come! Read yourself some epic stories in the stars – if you can still find any! Sign your name heroically in the brooding darkness, if that's what it takes! But when it reaches you, little man . . . When it reaches you . . ."

I let the phone fall from my hand and shatter on the rough stone.

Here I am, I thought, holding a tender thing in my shivering fingers. Here I am, alone with the deepest and most vulnerable of all loves, letting it sink beneath my arms, carving a bottomless hole in my final embrace . . .

over and over and over.

Overhead, those burning sky lights were crawling out of the torn sky fabric. Huge lightning jellyfish were drifting through the night. Moonbeams were twisting and swirling in their presence . . .

drawing me back from every retreat I have ever made, every missed opportunity, every failed adventure . . .

drawing me back from every magnificent disappointment for one last insatiable hug.

Time and time again, I had found myself running away screaming from all the world's alleged opportunities, terrified by the unspeakable beauty of being a small thing trying to stare all that restless floating spectacle in the face.

Time and time again, it was gentle, unspoken things that pulled me back from my own abyss, even as they threatened to crack open the sky with their impossible tenderness.

Now here they were, claiming their home back from a billion hiding places . . . and somehow making me whole in the process.

No more boxes demanding to be ticked. No more eyes looking me up and down.

No more mean little envelopes pouring through letterboxes.

No more walls and doors and windows, looking through each other.

No more quiet unseen floods, breaking my soul like a river axe driving its way through dead rock.

No more small fears.

There we were, watching the sky darken, listening to the eerie sounds of a dark thing growling over the sky, waiting for it to swallow us.

But now, as I watch the eerie march of the lightning masters . . .

as I feel their torch-lit tentacles splitting open the darkness, even as it looms over everything . . . as the dance of a billion sacred psychedelic wonders begins to make its presence known . . .

as I stand like a tiny beach pebble in their path, holding something so delicately woven, it cannot possibly hope to save me . . .

This is the first time I have ever felt complete.

The noise of a dark thing has come and gone, in a flurry of massive dinosaur jellyfish and a tide of lightning.

I stand impossibly vulnerable in its path, just as I have always done, as though something that seeped out through bones and tear ducts alike was always preparing me for this moment –

as though this act alone means everything.

The page where the geese go

I wrote a little picture book, and I had been carrying it halfway across the country, looking for somewhere to put it.

I wasn't sure where it would fit, seeing as this was a book for nobody. I knew as soon as I started doodling it that none of the somebodies would like it. They all had good reasons to still be somebody. They were all super motivated and awesome – or at least, that's what their taglines said.

But I wasn't looking for anybody. I certainly wasn't looking for somebody. I was looking for nobody, which is why I wrote the book.

That's the thing – I really had *written* it. It was a picture book, to be sure, but every one of those doodles was a word – a scribble as much as a sketch . . .

I'd written all the lost words . . . the ones we couldn't say anymore . . . into a book.

Maybe I'd written it for someone I hadn't met yet – someone who would hold me tight and hug my giggles back out of the margins.

Maybe I'd simply written it for me – for all that was left of me.

As I wandered the lines where the trains used to run, the sprawling railyard exercise book where the cities used to do their homework, the air was thick with decay. Old words, flapping like beached fish, gasping for mercy in the dryness.

Got no drumbeat in this water,

sang the book.

Got no rhythm in these waves. Got no dance left.

Got no flight.

Got no air left in these wings.

I had written watchtowers and cameras into this book. I'd launched satellites across its pages and written them into orbit.

Every time I cried, the book would bathe in my tears, flicking its pages through the curtains of waterfall. Sometimes it would dance there, showering me with my own wet release.

But suddenly, there are no more tracks to follow. No more ghostly train carriages. No more application forms written out across the railway pages.

Suddenly, the world that absolutely did not want me here has vanished – almost as if it had suddenly realised it didn't actually want anyone at all. Not even itself.

Apparently, worlds can be like that.

So I am lying on the banks of a river as it carves new words into the pit of the sky. Lightning words.

Suddenly, the clouds and I seem to be on the same page again, whittling the last vestiges of starlight into kindling. The lightning rivers are glowing with our fires, and huge flocks of phantom geese are gathering around the flames, whirling and swooping and stirring the fierce colours . . .

painting the sunset with their plaintive screeches . . . writing vibrant new moons out of heartbreak –

blue moons, red moons, yellow moons, purple moons –

and launching them into space.

I'm crying at the sheer scale of it, and new books are leaping out of the waterfalls, desperate to join the great scribble festival in the sky.

I am hurt and aching and lost . . . and far too exhausted to add much to the poetry they are writing. But perhaps my tears are finally speaking for themselves. Perhaps the galactic geese are sending their message further than I could have hoped.

Faerie spin

I was walking through dead weights. Dragging.

I was dragging a heavy place behind me – and sometimes it was all I could do to stand in it.

I was waiting for the chance to float, to lift myself out of the coldness and hover. However icy the sky might look, however frosty its doorways into outer space, it couldn't possibly be as cold as it is down here.

I needed a touch.

I needed one of those magical touches that fizzes deep between my truth and my imagination –

like a fuse, lit across places that only exist when something . . . or someone . . . has opened up the pit of yearning in my soul.

Insatiable,

but somehow never for the things on offer.

I needed a friend, a reckless benevolence of some kind, to swoop down and rescue me – much like the helicopter that a teacher once told me was never going to come.

Back then, just one right answer would have been enough to save me. Now, of course, right answers are the least of my concerns.

More often than not, I still seem to find myself waiting for clouds:

small, hybrid clouds, halfway between street and sky, like billowy faeries.

They swoop in from the breezy river of lost love, darting around like kites on broken strings until I catch them. There they dissolve between my fingers, leaving me waiting for the one billow faerie I haven't found yet – the one that will spread out like an orange fire at sunset, warmed and refreshed by my grip, spreading its wings like a manta ray and swimming me home among the stars.

I know it's there. I see it on occasion, skirting the outer rim of my dreams – a vast, rich, impossibly textured thing, like a squadron of mossy carpets, frisking the cosmic pillars for warmth, fed by the stories from a gazillion unseen shores.

The trees are light years tall, their leaves burning in high pillars where stars are born.

In many ways, however, it's a far tinier, more intimate creature. It's a hand on my skin, a vague weepy tingle of something that was not there before.

A shapeshifter.

I felt one of these transformations not so long ago.

I watched a small, wounded thing crawl out onto a stage and reach up for the only road available –

a lone trapeze, hanging from some high place in the dark.

Her hands took shape around the bar, and as she pulled, the

rest of her body followed suit. I watched her hang like stardust in the air.

Her limbs swirled and twitched and stretched in my spotlight – a lonely octopus, swatched in glowing plankton;

a girl, sitting on the gentle edge of forever.

I saw the room light up around her as she swung round and round the rope, weaving all my stray tears like a water wheel.

When she finally slid back down to earth, she walked like an angel through the applause. I followed her through the tunnel of curtains.

Offstage, out of her sparkly costume, she walked like a broken thing – like me.

I want a costume like that, I thought, so that when being the boy in the cold faerie place becomes unbearable, I could become the girl who spins galaxies from a static trapeze . . . or the cloud who swims between moonbeams and finds unborn shores there.

Hug Station "Dandelion"

Yeah, yeah . . .

I know the world has been making love without me.

I saw pictures.

But me,

I

like

hugs . . .

the kind where you dive in

and scrunch yourself up

into that warm,

shiny place

where someone else is holding you

as though

everything they've ever been

has come home to this moment . . .

as though

they're never going to let you go.

I like the hugs

where one sacred moment

has been stitched into all of our spirals,

catching our spirits as we fall

into the fabric of waiting . . .

into the fabric of space.

I like to cuddle with warm, teary rain,

melting my fingers

deep into all of those moon-dusted cracks,

tearing the fabric of

massive cosmic nebulae

and icy,

horizonless,

star-torched chains –

spilling my passions

over all of the clockwork of galaxy floors.

I like to melt between raindrops,

down into all of those traumatized cracks

where sadness falls in cosmic rays,

stealing the orbit

of battered cosmic stone . . .

weaving spells between their equations

and hiding in the chilly hinterlands between their laws.

I like to adopt smog rings

and smoke puppies

from the fume nurseries on the shallow edge of mighty roads,

saving their shivering, shellshocked ears

from the

stalling and swearing

of over-stressed traffic.

I make love to the warm air in subway tunnels,

where fugitive shooting stars hide

from the terror of emptiness.

We ride each other between the signals,

watching the trains

vacuum up the end-of-day crowds.

We make ticket machines moan

with the thrill of train beams

germinating in darkness

and we stretch our ecstatic hands over the timetables.

Travel cards

shred themselves with shame

at the clarity of our passion,

floating off like fluffy seeds

and drifting our love back to platform 4b.

Like dandelion seeds,

waiting to re-colonize the starscape.

I like to cuddle,

until every little

finger-skating

ripple of my hands

bears witness

to all the miracles we left on the road . . .

to all of those acid-hearted things

that mattered so much in the margins

and never showed up on the bill.

Pixie pilot

The deeper in I drifted, the more comfortable the textures became.

Bubbles and rugs of soft moss, blanketing bough bark and tree stump alike. Fern fronds, wafting against my legs. Dew-sprinkled lichen, shining tiny rainbows across the branches.

Forest things, touched by the benevolence of drifting spirits.

This was my first time. I didn't have the precision wings of the faerie folk. I couldn't swoop and soar like they could. I couldn't hover.

All I could do was roll and drift on the misty currents of the forest floor as they caught the billow of my little pleated skirt.

Still, the trees seemed to revel in my company. Twig-joint fingers drifted over my skin, sniffing the subtly coloured air, frisking the multicultural swirls of spore for new stories, breathing in the excitement of discovery. Overhead, bright red berries began to explode in vibrant splatters of celebration.

It was quite some time since I had felt so joyous, or so complete – like coming home to find that all my travels had somehow been irrelevant . . . and that most genuine and benevolent spells continued to stand their own ground, even when it seemed as if all such magic had long-since been abolished.

The only thing that really mattered here was things that stretched and reached, like a hand desperate to stop somebody from falling or a heart desperate to touch something precious before it flies away. Yes, the only thing that mattered here was branches and roots and things that stretched into the bottomless core of things.

They spread themselves out like scribbled notelets in a margin, chasing the clouds and capturing the sun, just as the leaf-roof canopy had re-woven the sky from creamy blue to mottled green. Even the atmosphere was alive here, in a way I had somehow forgotten, back in the land of small spaces and huge terrors.

I felt like a machine in their grip, rusted and somehow gentler than before.

I traced the curve of a gnarled mossy limb as it spiraled over me, reading secret combinations etched into the bark and wondering what kind of treasures were hidden there, perhaps hoping the poetry of piracy would lift me.

As it turned out, my pixie skirt was doing fine on its own.

There were cogs and gears and rotor blades woven through its pleats, whirring and and stirring with each bounce and roll. My thighs bled away and my old skin crumbled as the soft, powdery fullness of my own benevolence settled over the mist in assorted woody flavours.

Leaning against the nearest tree trunk, I hugged myself into crinkle-fluffed bark, baptising my arms with as much green fairy dust as I could gather.

The tree hugged me back, pulling on the unseen levers that had stitched themselves into the seams of my skirt. Unraveling the little pixie robot. Twisting and turning me like a toy doll. I could feel my thighs begin to bruise against the hidden ratchets in the atmosphere, climbing me higher than I had thought possible up to that point.

Suddenly, I felt a wave of springs releasing themselves up and down my body, leaving an intoxicating lightness in their wake. I could, I fancied, have stitched my name clear through the leaf-broken sky, had the forest so wished – perhaps weaving my new face into some berry-lit nebula where only the bravest of birds dare nest.

I began to remember the person I used to be, before the world had filed it away beneath an avalanche of angry, bitter, petty things – harsh, merciless, endlessly demanding numbers and unbearable silences where the air used to whisper into my soul.

I remembered myself, writing stories through the rivers of raindrop on a bedroom window . . . imagining strange wet engineers in the puddles outside . . . crying with the despair nobody was supposed to admit to.

Now, suddenly, I was a thing of hope . . . a clockwork doll . . . a music box, bursting into red-berry fireworks.

I remembered the tears . . . and the rain . . . and I found myself crying again as the beautiful mechanics of pixie flight reasserted themselves around me and through me.

I cried.

The tree cried. The forest cried.

Red berries continued to explode overhead, and I found myself
swirling up to join them – a fragile pleated thing, rewriting
the wobbly shape of hope on a plume of powdery blue-green
benevolence.

The tingle of stars and sea monsters

Y'know,

giving up should look like something . . . like something sacred

and otherworldly.

Giving up should look like you, cloud of clouds,

monster of monsters,

master of hot spicy tentacles. Giving up should look like I did, standing in the rain

in my inappropriate clothing,

still dressed for the hard grey streets I had run away from.

I had nothing left but my desperation,

my aching need for some unspoken revelation, thrumming like some strange interstellar engine – like the the warp drives of space geese,

heading home in v-shaped squadrons,

sweeping their silhouettes over the still-burning horizon. They follow the tide to new worlds.

You follow the tide because the ocean is all you have ever known.

You might as well have been dumping all the seas of the world on me that day, as I stood beneath wave after wave of raindrops. I didn't care how soaked I was. I didn't care how much of the mountain you washed loose around my feet. I didn't care because I had given up.

This should look like something, I remember thinking, tragic and twisted though the moment felt.

For all my sense of failure and defeat, this was a moment far too precious to remain unmarked.

It shouldn't hide in the nurturing darkness, beneath the vast billowy tentacles of a sea monster.

It should blossom

like a pollen-driven star,

pirouetting its petals through space.

It should say something, if only to the sky –

a silent thing, with no point to make, hovering with the love of something only really seen when the light goes out.

Giving up should shine a moment, I thought, instead of dying behind these eyes, where the door closes ever so softly to keep the stillness in . . .

and sometimes to leave the best of us locked away.

But there were no locked doors here, in this momentous land of giant floating sea monsters and rain-soaked runaways.

There was simply me, standing forever in the rain.

It does something to a soul when the mountains appear, heaving themselves roughly but beautifully from the bright wet fabric. Walls of stone, towering over the wetlands, glowering down from the mist in triumph.

Everything I had been running from began to die there – including me. But even with the pain still gnawing at my soul, I was far too exhilarated to want to save myself.

It was a place of cascading waterways and torn peat rugs, whose loose threads would occasionally erupt into tangled tree limbs and lush, mossy woodland; wild streams, dancing over furry green rocks; raindrops and tree roots chasing each other through deep cracks in the dark peaty floor of the Universe.

It was a place for all those broken things who could no longer breathe properly in the harsh streets and mean little rooms.

A place, perhaps, for me, I hoped . . . the spirit that stands in heavy rain and waits for sea monsters.

That's what you used to be, I thought, watching you swirl and growl over the high peaks.

I imagined you back in some deep ocean trench, frisking the floor of the abyss for meals. You were the leviathan there – the apex predator, prowling the waters around the smoke stacks, where eerie pillars of primeval smoke rose up from somewhere deep within the world's heart.

I imagined the day you swam too close, and a burst of warm smoke sent you tumbling upwards.

Freed from the huge pressures of the deep, you stretched and grew until, on reaching the surface, your vaporous body floated out of the water, joining the vast cargo crowds in their long-distance monsoon runs.

That's how I imagined you, as you could yourself around the mountains and your tentacles wove misty illusions through the valleys.

"This," whispered the saturated air, "is what monsters really look like." A crown of river water carving fresh gullies down the mountainside.

A galaxy made of raindrops, bouncing over my sodden clothes.

A sea of fern hands waving at me from every crumbling log, every tree stump. "I can't leave this place," I thought.

"I can't leave this place, where even the stars themselves are melting, just to lean closer.

"I can't leave this place where leviathans play, melting their own laughter with the breath of dragons and stroking my shoulders with their gentle, billowy hands.

"Just keep standing here," the rain whispered back.

"Even when your shoes and your heart are sodden beyond repair, just keep standing in the rain."

My stomach was tingling with the fear of all the places I didn't want to be, all the things that kept threatening to steal me away and tear me apart, tingling through the rain-bitten core of me as I wept.

The rainwater was coming from monsters far, far bigger than I was. The tears were etching themselves into high mountain stone.

But I was the one who was crying.

I was crying and tingling from my soaked hood to my soaked shoes, and the tingle was changing everything.

It was a rollercoaster tingle, just like the relentless mountain rain.

One moment, it was the tingle of euphoria as I soaked in the stunning textures all around me; next it was the shredding claws of fear and guilt and self-loathing, poured into me from the echoes of harsh, accusatory voices.

But none of that mattered. Only the rain mattered here, as the floodgates of several worlds continued to burst open over my head. As far as this rich, rain-woven tingle was concerned, every one of these feelings was precious beyond measure. As far as my tingling, spiraling soul was concerned, they all spoke the same message – my need to be held.

My need to share the plumes of exultation . . .

My need to share the drumbeat of rain stars on my imagination . . . My need to be hugged and cuddled in my desperation . . .

My need to be loved through all those cold, scary, twisted places . . . all those places that matter so, so much . . .

My need to be held – that was the message, tingling inside me, no matter how high the mountains or how cold the rain or how huge the monster.

So I did the only thing I could. I let the fear take me. I let it claw me . . . and I waited, breathless and tingling, on the rainswept river valley beneath the monsters and the mountains, as one sacred voice dived into my churning pit of horrors and treasures, weaving its beautifully terrifying tingle into the swirling galaxy of raindrops I had become.

This, I realized, was my wild new safe place, hugging me home, through the middle of things that always feel inconsolable.

This was the safe place that would never, ever be safe. But only here would the leviathans and the oceans and the star-spun galaxies gather around me. Only here would the hug feel real and wet and breathlessly, Impossibly exciting.

And all sorts of voices would doubtlessly try to shrink it and define it and frame it before my walk through the rain was over.

But the sky would know, and so would I.

Milton Keynes UK
Ingram Content Group UK Ltd.
UKHW020850280424
441864UK00010B/165